Olesia Naumchyk

MOST FASCINATING AND UNUSUAL CHRISTMAS TRADITIONS AROUND THE WORLD

A Journey Through the World's Most Unusual Christmas Traditions

Introduction:

Christmas, a holiday celebrated in many parts of the world, comes with an astonishing variety of traditions. From the haunting figure of Krampus in Austria to the playful Yule Lads in Iceland, each culture has unique ways of marking this special time of year. Some customs are centuries old, steeped in folklore and ancient rituals, while others have evolved more recently but are no less fascinating. In this book, we embark on a journey to explore of the most unusual, interesting, and heartwarming Christmas traditions from across the globe.

Table of Contents:

Introduction: The Diversity of Christmas Traditions

Chapter 1: Europe's Christmas Marvels – 1

Chapter 2: Latin American Christmas Celebrations – 13

- Las Posadas (Mexico)
- Noche de Rábanos (Oaxaca, Mexico)
- Venezuelan Roller Skating to Church (Caracas, Venezuela)
- Christmas Fireworks (El Salvador)
- Paradura del Niño (Venezuela)
- Argentina's Fire Lanterns
- Christmas in the Andes (Peru)
- The Nativity Play Tradition (Colombia)
- Midnight Mass, La Misa de Gallo (Peru)
- Giant Christmas Lantern Festival (Philippines)

- Ethiopian Orthodox Christmas (Ethiopia)
- Christmas Carnivals (Nigeria)
- Fasting Before Christmas (Eritrea)
- Christmas Beach Celebrations (Ghana)
- Midnight Processions (Congo)
- Christmas Dance Celebrations (Zimbabwe)
- Kwanzaa and Its Pan-African Influence
- Asian Christmas Surprises
- KFC for Christmas Dinner (Japan)
- The Floating Christmas Lanterns (Thailand)
- Christmas and Cricket (India)
- Chinese Winter Solstice Celebrations (China)
- South Korean Christmas Festivities
- Philippines' Simbang Gabi
- Giving Oranges as Gifts (China)
- Tió de Nadal (Andorra)
- Christmas Bread and Wine (India)
- Santa's Footprints (Japan)

CHAPTER 1:

Europe's Christmas Marvels

Europe is home to some of the world's most diverse and intriguing Christmas traditions. From spooky folklore figures like Krampus to the warm glow of St. Lucia's Day in Sweden, European countries offer a rich array of customs that range from whimsical and heartwarming to downright strange. Let's take a closer look at 20 of the most fascinating and unusual Christmas traditions across Europe.

1. Krampus (Austria, Germany)

In the Alpine regions of Austria and Germany, the fearsome figure of Krampus roams the streets in early December. A stark contrast to the kindly St. Nicholas, Krampus is a horned, devil-like creature who punishes naughty children. Dressed in terrifying masks and costumes, participants parade through towns in Krampuslauf (Krampus run), frightening both children and adults into good behavior. This dark side of Christmas serves as a reminder to children to stay on Santa's "nice" list.

2. The Yule Goat (Sweden)

In Sweden, the Yule Goat has ancient roots, originally symbolizing a creature that demanded gifts rather than delivering them. Nowadays, one of the most famous representations is the Gävle Goat, a massive straw figure erected annually in the town of Gävle. It has gained notoriety for being the target of vandals who attempt to burn it down each year. Despite increased security, the goat has been successfully burned over 30 times since the tradition began in 1966.

3. St. Lucia's Day (Sweden)

Celebrated on December 13th, St. Lucia's Day is a significant part of Swedish Christmas tradition. Girls dress in white robes with red sashes, and the chosen "Lucia" wears a crown of candles on her head, symbolizing the return of light in the dark winter months. Lucia processions often take place in schools, churches, and homes, with the singing of traditional songs. This tradition honors St. Lucia, a Christian martyr, but also reflects ancient pagan celebrations of the winter solstice.

4. The Christmas Witch, La Befana (Italy)

In Italy, children look forward to a visit from La Befana, a kindly old witch who delivers gifts on the night of January 5th, Epiphany Eve. According to legend, La Befana was too busy to accompany the Wise Men to visit baby Jesus, and now she flies on her broomstick each year in search of him. Children leave out stockings for La Befana to fill with treats for the good and lumps of coal for the naughty.

5. Mari Lwyd (Wales)

The Welsh tradition of Mari Lwyd involves a group of people carrying a horse's skull draped in a white sheet, going from house to house singing and engaging in playful banter with the residents. The exchange is often in the form of a battle of wits or rhyming verses, after which the group is usually invited inside for food and drink. This eerie yet festive custom dates back centuries and is still practiced in some parts of Wales today.

6. The Caganer (Catalonia, Spain)

The Caganer is a small figurine of a man defecating, which Catalonians traditionally hide within nativity scenes. While it might seem strange or irreverent, the Caganer is considered a symbol of fertility and good luck, and adding him to the nativity is thought to ensure a bountiful year ahead. This quirky figure often takes on humorous forms, with modern versions representing famous figures from politics, sports, and pop culture.

7. Yule Lads (Iceland)

In Iceland, the Yule Lads—13 mischievous troll-like creatures—visit children in the 13 nights leading up to Christmas. Each Yule Lad has a distinct personality, such as Spoon-Licker, Door-Slammer, and Meat-Hook, and they leave gifts or rotting potatoes in the shoes that children place by the window. Icelandic folklore also includes Grýla, their terrifying mother, who punishes naughty children.

8. Christmas Markets (Germany)

Germany is renowned for its enchanting Christmas markets, known as Weihnachtsmärkte, which can be found in towns and cities throughout the country during the holiday season. These festive markets feature stalls selling handmade crafts, ornaments, and seasonal treats like glühwein (mulled wine), gingerbread, and sausages. The charming atmosphere, often accompanied by twinkling lights and carol singing, draws visitors from around the world.

9. Kiviak (Greenland)

In Greenland, Christmas feasts often include a unique delicacy called kiviak, which consists of small seabirds (called auks) that are fermented inside a sealskin for several months. Once sufficiently aged, the birds are consumed during festive occasions like Christmas. While this may sound unusual, kiviak is a traditional Inuit dish, and it is considered a special treat during the holiday season.

10. Wigilia and Opłatek (Poland)

In Poland, Christmas Eve is celebrated with Wigilia, a special meal that begins when the first star appears in the night sky. Families gather to share opłatek, a thin wafer that is broken and exchanged while offering good wishes. This tradition emphasizes unity and reconciliation. The Wigilia meal consists of 12 meatless dishes, symbolizing the 12 apostles, and often includes dishes like pierogi (dumplings) and barszcz (beet soup).

11. Shoes Instead of Stockings (Netherlands)

In the Netherlands, children place their shoes by the fireplace or windowsill on the night of December 5th, eagerly awaiting a visit from Sinterklaas (St. Nicholas). If they've been good, they'll find their shoes filled with gifts and sweets the next morning. Children often leave carrots or hay for Sinterklaas' horse, who accompanies him on his journey.

12. Burning the Yule Log (France)

In parts of France, the ancient tradition of burning the Yule log still exists, symbolizing warmth, light, and the hope for a prosperous new year. In some regions, families would bring in a large log, often from a fruit tree, and burn it slowly over several days. The ashes were believed to bring good luck for the coming year, and this custom has evolved into the more modern tradition of the Bûche de Noël, a yule log-shaped cake.

13. Père Noël and Père Fouettard (France)

In France, Père Noël is the kind and generous figure who delivers gifts to children, but he is often accompanied by Père Fouettard, a darker figure who carries a whip to punish naughty children. Père Noël is celebrated on Christmas Eve, and children leave out their shoes to be filled with presents if they've been good.

14. Boxing Day (UK)

The day after Christmas, December 26th, is known as Boxing Day in the UK. Historically, it was a day when employers gave their workers "Christmas boxes" containing gifts or bonuses. Today, Boxing Day is known for shopping, sports, and spending time with family. It also has a charitable aspect, with people donating to those in need.

15. Feast of St. Nicholas (Germany)

On the night of December 5th, German children leave out their shoes in anticipation of St. Nicholas' Feast Day. If they've been good, St. Nicholas fills the shoes with gifts, fruit, and candy, while naughty children may find a twig or a lump of coal.

16. The Star Singers (Poland)

In Poland, groups of Star Singers go door-to-door during the Christmas season, singing carols and carrying a large star that represents the Star of Bethlehem. These singers spread joy and blessings while collecting donations for charitable causes.

17. Yule Buck (Norway)

In Norway, the Yule Buck or Julbukk tradition involves people dressing up in costumes and going door to door, singing carols or performing short plays. The hosts offer treats in return, and it's a fun way to bring the community together during the holiday season.

18. Christmas Carp in the Bathtub (Slovakia)

In Slovakia and other parts of Central Europe, it's traditional to eat carp for Christmas dinner. In the days leading up to Christmas, the fish is often kept alive in the family's bathtub until it's time to cook it. This custom is part of the region's rich Christmas Eve meal, which includes various symbolic foods.

19. Christmas Porridge (Finland)

In Finland, it's customary to serve a special rice porridge called Joulupuuro on Christmas morning. Hidden inside the porridge is an almond, and the person who finds the almond is said to have good luck for the coming year. This simple yet heartwarming tradition adds an element of fun and surprise to the family meal.

These European traditions highlight the diversity and rich cultural heritage that shape how Christmas is celebrated across the continent. From fearsome folklore figures to light-filled processions, each custom reflects the unique history and beliefs of its country, offering a glimpse into the many ways people come together to celebrate the magic of the season.

CHAPTER 2:

Latin American Christmas Celebrations

Christmas in Latin America is a rich tapestry of religious rituals, lively festivals, and unique customs deeply rooted in the region's diverse cultural history. From reenacting Mary and Joseph's search for shelter to dazzling fireworks displays, these traditions offer a vivid glimpse into how the Christmas spirit is celebrated across Latin American countries.

1. Las Posadas (Mexico)

Las Posadas is one of Mexico's most cherished Christmas traditions, celebrated from December 16th to 24th. This nine-day event reenacts the journey of Mary and Joseph as they search for shelter before the birth of Jesus. Each night, participants form a procession, visiting different homes where they sing traditional songs asking for "posada" (shelter). The hosts of the final house invite the group inside for prayers, music, and festive celebrations. The night usually ends with a piñata filled with treats for the children, symbolizing the reward for perseverance.

2. Noche de Rábanos (Oaxaca, Mexico)

On December 23rd, the town of Oaxaca celebrates Noche de Rábanos (The Night of the Radishes), an incredibly unique festival where radishes are carved into intricate nativity scenes and other Christmas-related figures. Local artisans create elaborate displays using these vegetables, and the best creations are awarded prizes. Though radishes might seem like an odd medium for art, this tradition has been celebrated for over a century and attracts visitors from all over the world.

3. Roller Skating to Church (Caracas, Venezuela)

In Caracas, Venezuela, one of the most unusual Christmas traditions is roller skating to church for early morning mass on Christmas Eve. Streets are closed off to traffic, allowing people to skate safely to attend the Misa de Aguinaldo (Christmas mass). The tradition is fun for families and friends, and it has become a beloved and quirky part of Caracas' Christmas celebration.

4. Christmas Fireworks (El Salvador)

In El Salvador, the Christmas season is lit up with vibrant fireworks displays. Starting on Christmas Eve, Salvadorans set off fireworks as part of the celebration, lighting up the night sky. Children and adults alike enjoy this noisy and colorful tradition, and fireworks can be seen and heard throughout the country well into Christmas Day.

5. Paradura del Niño (Venezuela)

In Venezuela, the Paradura del Niño is a unique celebration held on January 1st or any time in January. It is a religious event that celebrates the standing up of the Baby Jesus, a symbolic moment when the figure of baby Jesus is "stood" up in the nativity scene after his birth. The community gathers to carry the statue of the infant Jesus in a joyful procession, accompanied by music and prayers. This tradition is often seen in Venezuelan homes and churches and reflects the community's deep reverence for the nativity.

6. Argentina's Fire Lanterns

In Argentina, the night sky on Christmas Eve is illuminated by globos, or fire lanterns. These paper lanterns, filled with candles, are released into the air, creating a magical sight. Families gather to release their globos after their Nochebuena (Christmas Eve dinner), often accompanying the moment with fireworks. The glowing lanterns symbolize hopes and wishes for the coming year.

7. Christmas in the Andes (Peru)

In Peru, particularly in the Andean regions, Christmas is a vibrant fusion of indigenous customs and Catholic traditions. One of the most important aspects of the holiday is the crafting of retablos, which are intricate wooden boxes filled with figurines depicting nativity scenes and local life. On Christmas Eve, many families attend La Misa de Gallo (Midnight Mass), and markets known as Santuranticuy in Cusco sell beautiful handmade decorations and religious art, often featuring llamas or alpacas instead of donkeys.

8. The Nativity Play Tradition (Colombia)

In Colombia, nativity plays or pastorelas are a popular part of the Christmas season. These plays often involve children dressed as angels, shepherds, and the Three Wise Men, reenacting the story of the birth of Jesus. Many towns and cities host public nativity plays, and the performances are full of joy, music, and community spirit. After the play, the celebration often continues with aguinaldos, small gifts exchanged among loved ones.

9. Midnight Mass, La Misa de Gallo (Peru)

In Peru, La Misa de Gallo (The Rooster's Mass) is an important tradition on Christmas Eve. The name refers to the rooster that is said to have crowed on the night Jesus was born. Families attend this midnight mass, where the birth of Jesus is celebrated with prayer and joyful hymns. After the service, families return home to a festive meal featuring traditional Peruvian dishes like lechón (roast pork) and panetón (a sweet bread filled with candied fruit).

10. Giant Christmas Lantern Festival (Philippines)

Though geographically outside of Latin America, the Giant Lantern Festival in the Philippines deserves mention due to the shared cultural heritage. The Parol (lantern) is a symbol of the Filipino Christmas spirit, representing the Star of Bethlehem. The city of San Fernando hosts the Ligligan Parul, or Giant Lantern Festival, where enormous, intricately designed parols are displayed, lit by thousands of lights. The festival has become so iconic that San Fernando is known as the "Christmas Capital of the Philippines."

CHAPTER 3:

African Festive Traditions

Christmas in Africa is celebrated with rich cultural diversity, blending Christian religious traditions with local customs. From lively dance festivals to beach celebrations, these festivities showcase the unique ways different African nations embrace the holiday season. This chapter explores seven fascinating Christmas traditions across Africa.

1. Ethiopian Orthodox Christmas (Ethiopia)

In Ethiopia, Christmas is celebrated on January 7th according to the Julian calendar, and is known as Ganna. Ethiopian Orthodox Christians begin their day by attending church services that start early in the morning, often before dawn. The faithful wear traditional white robes, called shamma, as they attend mass, which is filled with prayer, music, and the chanting of hymns. After the service, families gather for a feast, where they enjoy traditional Ethiopian dishes like doro wat (spicy chicken stew) served with injera (flatbread). Ganna is a time of fasting, prayer, and community, with the holiday spirit deeply rooted in faith.

2. Christmas Carnivals (Nigeria)

In Nigeria, Christmas is a lively and colorful celebration, especially in cities like Calabar, where the Calabar Carnival is held. Known as "Africa's biggest street party," this month-long festival in December culminates in a grand parade around Christmas time. The streets come alive with music, dance, and vibrant costumes as locals and tourists gather to enjoy the spectacle. Parades feature elaborate floats, and performers engage in lively displays of Afrobeat music and traditional dance. While the carnival is secular in nature, it plays a significant role in bringing people together to celebrate the joy of the season.

3. Fasting Before Christmas (Eritrea)

In Eritrea, like Ethiopia, Christmas is celebrated on January 7th by followers of the Eritrean Orthodox Church. The lead-up to Christmas involves a period of fasting, known as Tsome Nehase, which lasts for 43 days. During this time, devout Christians abstain from meat, dairy, and other animal products, focusing on spiritual reflection and preparation for the birth of Christ. On Christmas Day, the fast is broken with a feast, where families gather to enjoy traditional dishes such as zigni (a spicy meat stew) and injera. This period of fasting and prayer reinforces the spiritual significance of Christmas for Eritreans.

4. Christmas Beach Celebrations (Ghana)

In Ghana, Christmas is a time for family, friends, and community, and one of the most popular ways to celebrate is through beach gatherings. After attending church services, many Ghanaians head to the coast to enjoy the warm weather with picnics, music, and games. Beaches are filled with families celebrating Christmas together, and it's not uncommon to see people dancing to lively highlife music or engaging in friendly soccer matches. Ghanaian Christmas meals often include jollof rice, fufu, and stews made with chicken or goat, reflecting the festive and communal nature of the season.

5. Midnight Processions (Congo)

In the Democratic Republic of the Congo, Christmas Eve is marked by elaborate midnight processions, where churchgoers march through the streets singing hymns and carols. These processions are often led by children dressed as angels or shepherds, carrying candles or lanterns to symbolize the light of Christ. After the processions, the congregation gathers for a special midnight mass. Christmas in the Congo is deeply rooted in religious observance, with the processions serving as a way for communities to express their faith and joy during the holiday season.

6. Christmas Dance Celebrations (Zimbabwe)

In Zimbabwe, Christmas is a time for music and dance, and one of the most exciting traditions is the Christmas dance celebration known as the Jiti Dance. After attending church services, families and communities come together for outdoor gatherings that often feature traditional dances accompanied by drumming and singing. The Jiti Dance, in particular, is a high-energy, joyful dance that involves quick footwork and is often performed at family gatherings. Food also plays a central role in Zimbabwean Christmas, with families preparing large feasts that include roasted meats, maize, and vegetables. The combination of faith, music, and communal celebration makes Christmas in Zimbabwe a vibrant and lively affair.

7. Kwanzaa and Its Pan-African Influence

While Kwanzaa is not a traditional African holiday, its roots lie in African heritage and culture, and it has a growing influence across the African diaspora, including Africa itself. Kwanzaa is celebrated from December 26th to January 1st and was created in the 1960s by Dr. Maulana Karenga as a way to honor African culture, community, and values. The seven-day festival emphasizes the Nguzo Saba (Seven Principles), which include unity, self-determination, and cooperative economics. During Kwanzaa, participants light candles on the Kinara, discuss the principles, and reflect on their cultural heritage. While primarily observed in the United States, Kwanzaa has spread to parts of Africa and is seen as a celebration of Pan-African identity and pride.

Christmas in Africa is a time for faith, community, and vibrant celebrations. Whether it's through the spiritual reflection of fasting in Eritrea, the joyful dances in Zimbabwe, or the grand carnivals in Nigeria, the holiday season brings people together in meaningful and diverse ways. These traditions highlight the unique ways that African cultures honor the spirit of Christmas, blending local customs with Christian practices, and emphasizing the values of family, community, and joy.

CHAPTER 4:

Asian Christmas Surprises

Asia, with its diverse cultures and traditions, offers some of the most unique and fascinating ways to celebrate Christmas. From fast food feasts in Japan to floating lanterns in Thailand, Asian Christmas celebrations blend religious customs, modern influences, and local traditions in truly delightful ways. Let's explore some of the surprising ways Christmas is observed across Asia.

1. KFC for Christmas Dinner (Japan)

One of the most surprising and well-known Christmas traditions in Japan is eating KFC for Christmas dinner. This tradition began in the 1970s with a marketing campaign called "Kentucky for Christmas," which suggested KFC as a convenient alternative to a traditional Western-style Christmas meal. Since then, it has become so popular that many Japanese families pre-order their KFC Christmas meals weeks in advance. This meal often includes fried chicken, cake, and even champagne, making it a festive way to celebrate Christmas in a country where the holiday is more commercial than religious.

2. The Floating Christmas Lanterns (Thailand)

In predominantly Buddhist Thailand, Christmas is not widely celebrated as a religious holiday, but some regions incorporate floating lantern festivals into their seasonal celebrations. The tradition of Loy Krathong, a festival where people release floating lanterns onto water, has been adapted in some places to celebrate Christmas. These glowing lanterns symbolize letting go of negativity and welcoming new hopes, blending Buddhist and Western customs. In tourist-heavy areas like Bangkok and Chiang Mai, Christmas decorations and festive events are common, with the floating lanterns adding a beautiful, symbolic twist to the holiday.

3. Christmas and Cricket (India)

In India, Christmas, known as Bada Din ("Big Day"), is a joyful celebration, especially for Christian communities. One surprising tradition in many regions of India is the association between Christmas and cricket, the country's most popular sport. Families and communities often gather to play cricket on Christmas Day after attending church services. In Goa and other regions with large Christian populations, churches are decorated with poinsettias, and homes are lit with star-shaped lanterns. Traditional Indian Christmas sweets like kulkuls and neureos are shared, blending local flavors with Western customs.

4. Chinese Winter Solstice Celebrations (China)

In China, where Christmas is not a traditional holiday, the Winter Solstice Festival (also known as Dongzhi) is celebrated around the same time. Families come together to share meals, with dishes like tangyuan (glutinous rice balls) symbolizing reunion and harmony. Though Christmas is becoming more popular in major cities, where shopping malls and restaurants put up festive decorations, the focus for many Chinese families remains on Winter Solstice, a deeply traditional holiday that marks the return of longer days and the hope for prosperity.

5. South Korean Christmas Festivities

South Korea is one of the few Asian countries where Christmas is an official public holiday due to the significant Christian population. Church services play a central role in Christmas celebrations, with many churches holding midnight masses and offering special Christmas events. South Korean Christmas customs often blend Western traditions, with people exchanging gifts, decorating trees, and even dressing up as Santa Claus. A unique South Korean twist is the emphasis on couple's activities, as Christmas is seen as a romantic holiday, similar to Valentine's Day. Couples often go on dates, exchange gifts, and enjoy festive lights and ice skating.

6. Philippines' Simbang Gabi

In the Philippines, Christmas is one of the most important celebrations of the year, and the holiday season is known for being one of the longest in the world, starting as early as September. One of the most cherished Filipino Christmas traditions is Simbang Gabi, a series of nine dawn masses leading up to Christmas Eve. The faithful wake up early each morning from December 16th to 24th to attend mass in anticipation of Christmas Day. After the mass, people enjoy traditional foods like bibingka (rice cakes) and puto bumbong (purple rice cakes), which are sold outside churches. This tradition reflects the deep-rooted Catholic faith in the country.

7. Giving Oranges as Gifts (China)

In China, oranges are associated with prosperity and good fortune, and it is common to give oranges as gifts during Christmas and New Year celebrations. The word for "orange" sounds similar to the word for "wealth" in Mandarin, making oranges a symbol of good luck. While Christmas is not a national holiday, it is becoming increasingly commercialized in urban areas, with Christmas trees, lights, and gift exchanges becoming more common, especially among younger generations.

8. Tió de Nadal (Andorra)

Although geographically part of Europe, Andorra is a tiny country nestled between France and Spain with strong Catalan traditions, and it shares a unique Christmas custom with Catalonia. During the Christmas season, families in Andorra celebrate Tió de Nadal, also known as the Caga Tió. This tradition involves a hollow log with a painted face that children "feed" each night leading up to Christmas. On Christmas Eve, children hit the log with sticks, encouraging it to "poop" gifts and candies, much to their delight. While rooted in European tradition, Andorra's culture is distinct, blending both Catalan and French influences.

9. Christmas Bread and Wine (India)

In India, particularly in Christian communities, Christmas is celebrated with a traditional feast that often includes bread and wine, symbolizing unity and togetherness. After attending Midnight Mass, families share festive meals, where homemade wine and special breads like plum cake are served alongside dishes such as biryani and vindaloo. The mixing of Western Christmas traditions with local Indian cuisine reflects the diverse cultural influences that shape Indian Christmas celebrations, particularly in states like Kerala and Goa.

10. Santa's Footprints (Japan)

In Japan, where Christmas is celebrated more as a secular holiday, a unique custom for children involves Santa's footprints. Parents often leave flour or powder footprints around the house on Christmas Eve to "prove" that Santa visited during the night. Since gift-giving and family gatherings are central to the celebration, this small gesture adds a magical element to the holiday for children. As Christmas isn't a religious holiday in Japan, it focuses more on spreading joy, giving gifts, and creating festive memories.

Asian Christmas traditions showcase an incredible blend of influences, from Western commercialization to deeply rooted cultural and religious practices. Whether it's enjoying KFC in Japan, attending early morning Simbang Gabi masses in the Philippines, or celebrating Christmas with cricket matches in India, these customs reflect the region's adaptability and creativity in embracing the Christmas spirit. Each tradition adds its own cultural flavor to this global holiday, reminding us that while Christmas may look different across the world, its universal message of joy, togetherness, and hope remains strong.

CHAPTER 5:

North American Yuletide Wonders

Christmas in North America is a vibrant celebration that blends centuries-old traditions with modern, often quirky, customs. From festive parades to elaborate light displays, the Christmas spirit lights up towns and cities across the continent. In this chapter, we explore some of the most delightful and unique Christmas traditions celebrated across the USA, Canada, and Mexico.

1. The Christmas Pickle (USA)

A quirky American Christmas tradition involves hiding a pickle ornament deep within the Christmas tree. On Christmas morning, the first child to find the pickle receives an extra gift or is thought to have good luck for the year. While the origins of this tradition are somewhat unclear, many believe it was inspired by German customs, though most Germans are unfamiliar with it. Regardless of its true roots, the Christmas Pickle adds a fun scavenger hunt element to Christmas morning festivities.

2. Mummering (Canada)

In Newfoundland, Canada, the tradition of Mummering is a lively and unusual Christmas activity. Participants, called Mummers, dress in costumes and masks, disguising their identities, and go from house to house singing songs, dancing, and engaging in playful antics. The hosts try to guess who the Mummers are, and if they can't, the Mummers are invited in for drinks and treats. Mummering often takes place between Christmas and New Year's, and the lighthearted tradition brings communities together in celebration.

3. Poinsettias Everywhere (Mexico)

In Mexico, the Poinsettia—a bright red plant associated with Christmas—has become a national symbol of the holiday. The plant's origins date back to a Mexican legend about a poor girl who offered weeds to Jesus on Christmas Eve. Miraculously, the weeds bloomed into beautiful red flowers, now known as poinsettias, or "Nochebuena" in Spanish. Today, poinsettias are used to decorate homes, churches, and public spaces throughout Mexico during the holiday season.

4. Parades and Floats (USA)

In the USA, Christmas parades are a beloved tradition in many towns and cities. These parades feature elaborate floats, marching bands, and often a special appearance by Santa Claus himself. The Macy's Thanksgiving Day Parade in New York City, though held on Thanksgiving, is considered the unofficial start to the Christmas season, with its giant balloons, floats, and musical performances. Throughout December, local Christmas parades, such as the Hollywood Christmas Parade in Los Angeles and the Santa Claus Parade in Toronto, kick off the festive spirit in North America.

5. Christmas Light Competitions (USA)

Across the United States, neighborhoods get into the holiday spirit with Christmas light competitions. Homeowners adorn their houses and yards with dazzling displays of twinkling lights, inflatable snowmen, Santas, and even synchronized light shows set to music. These light competitions have become a fierce but friendly rivalry in many communities, with some families planning their elaborate displays months in advance. Popular competitions like the Dyker Heights Lights in Brooklyn, New York, and Candy Cane Lane in California draw visitors from near and far.

6. Christkindl Markets (USA)

Inspired by traditional German markets, Christkindl Markets have become popular in many U.S. cities, especially in areas with strong European influence. These festive outdoor markets, often held in cities like Chicago and Denver, offer handmade ornaments, festive foods like bratwurst and glühwein (mulled wine), and local crafts. Visitors can wander through the twinkling stalls, enjoy the holiday atmosphere, and pick up unique gifts. These markets are modeled after the famous Christkindlesmarkt in Nuremberg, Germany, bringing a bit of European charm to American cities.

7. Posh Christmas Crackers (UK, USA)

In both the UK and the USA, the tradition of pulling Christmas crackers during Christmas dinner has become a popular part of holiday celebrations. Christmas crackers are festively wrapped tubes that make a "pop" when pulled apart, revealing small gifts, jokes, and paper crowns. While the tradition originated in the UK, it has spread to the U.S. as a fun addition to Christmas feasts, particularly in homes with British heritage. Some families enjoy posh versions with high-quality treats, turning this into a fun and surprising moment of the holiday meal.

8. Christmas Boat Parades (USA)

In coastal regions of the U.S., especially in warmer states like Florida and California, Christmas boat parades are a spectacular tradition. Boats of all sizes, from small yachts to massive sailboats, are adorned with festive lights, decorations, and even animatronic Santas and reindeer. The boats parade through harbors and waterfronts, creating a stunning display of holiday cheer on the water. The Newport Beach Christmas Boat Parade in California is one of the most famous, attracting thousands of visitors each year to see the twinkling flotilla.

9. SantaCon (USA)

SantaCon is a modern Christmas tradition where people dress up as Santa Claus (or other holiday-themed characters) and gather in cities across the U.S. for a day of festive fun. SantaCon events usually involve bar crawls, charity fundraisers, and impromptu Christmas caroling. What started as a small event in San Francisco in the 1990s has grown into a global phenomenon, with major SantaCon gatherings in cities like New York, San Francisco, and Las Vegas. While it's mostly a lighthearted event, some cities have implemented guidelines to keep the revelry family-friendly.

10. New Orleans Christmas Lights and King Cakes (USA)

In New Orleans, Christmas is celebrated with the city's usual blend of festive spirit and cultural uniqueness. The Celebration in the Oaks at City Park is one of the most beautiful holiday light displays in the country, featuring millions of twinkling lights draped over the city's iconic oak trees. The festive season in New Orleans also includes King Cake—a traditional pastry associated with Epiphany (January 6th), but often enjoyed throughout the Christmas season. King Cake is a sweet, cinnamon-flavored cake decorated with green, gold, and purple sugar, and it contains a small plastic baby hidden inside. The person who finds the baby is said to have good luck and is expected to host the next party.

CHAPTER 6:

Oceanian Festive Oddities

Christmas in Oceania is shaped by the region's unique blend of tropical climates, island cultures, and a combination of Christian and indigenous traditions. The festive season often involves outdoor celebrations, delicious foods, and community gatherings that reflect the laid-back, joyful spirit of the islands. Let's take a look at some of the most interesting and unusual Christmas traditions in Australia, New Zealand, and the Pacific Islands.

1. Carols by Candlelight (Australia)

In Australia, where Christmas falls in the middle of summer, one of the most beloved traditions is Carols by Candlelight. Families gather in parks, stadiums, and open-air venues across the country on Christmas Eve to sing traditional Christmas carols by candlelight. The largest and most famous event takes place in Melbourne, where thousands of people gather at the Sidney Myer Music Bowl for a massive celebration, broadcast on television nationwide. The warm summer weather creates a unique atmosphere, with everyone singing together under the stars, holding candles that light up the night.

2. Pavlova and the Barbecue Tradition (New Zealand)

In New Zealand, Christmas is celebrated with a mix of traditional and local customs. A unique aspect of the Kiwi Christmas is the festive meal, which often includes a barbecue. Families gather outdoors to grill lamb, seafood, and sausages, taking full advantage of the summer weather. A quintessential New Zealand Christmas dessert is Pavlova, a meringue-based dish topped with whipped cream and fresh fruits like strawberries and kiwifruit. While Pavlova is also popular in Australia, New Zealanders proudly claim it as their own, and it remains a staple of the Christmas feast.

3. Christmas Island's Mass Crab Migration

One of the most unusual natural events associated with Christmas takes place on Christmas Island, an Australian territory in the Indian Ocean. Each year, millions of red crabs make their way from the island's forests to the ocean to spawn. The mass migration typically coincides with the start of the rainy season, which often occurs around Christmas time. Roads are closed, and locals take great care to protect the crabs as they cross paths, transforming the island into a spectacle of nature. Though not directly tied to the holiday, the timing of the migration makes it a fascinating feature of Christmas on the island.

4. Christmas on the Beach (Australia)

For many Australians, Christmas means celebrating on the beach. With temperatures soaring during the Southern Hemisphere's summer, families head to the coast to enjoy a sunny, relaxed Christmas Day. Beaches like Bondi in Sydney and St Kilda in Melbourne are packed with people enjoying barbecues, swimming, surfing, and beach games. Some families even bring their Christmas trees and decorations to the beach, turning it into an outdoor celebration. It's common to see Santa Claus dressed in swimwear or on a surfboard, adding a distinctively Aussie twist to the holiday.

5. Cook Islands' Unique Nativity Plays

In the Cook Islands, Christmas celebrations blend Christian traditions with local customs. A key part of the festivities is the staging of nativity plays, which are often performed outdoors and feature a mix of religious themes and island culture. The plays are lively and colorful, incorporating traditional songs and dances alongside the telling of the Christmas story. Community involvement is central to these performances, and nearly everyone in the village participates in some way, from acting to costume-making. These nativity plays emphasize the strong sense of community and faith that is central to Cook Islands Christmas celebrations.

6. Samoan White Sunday Celebrations

In Samoa, White Sunday is a major religious holiday celebrated in October, but its festive spirit extends into Christmas as well. During White Sunday, children are the focus of the celebrations, and they wear white clothes to symbolize purity. In December, the same community-driven spirit of faith continues with Christmas services, where children sing carols and recite Bible verses. Samoan Christmas gatherings often feature large feasts with dishes like umu (an earth oven meal), showcasing traditional Samoan hospitality and joy.

7. Island Choirs (Pacific Islands)

Throughout the Pacific Islands, Christmas choirs are an integral part of the holiday celebrations. In countries like Fiji, Tonga, and Samoa, community choirs rehearse for weeks leading up to Christmas, preparing to perform in churches, village squares, and homes. These choirs sing a mixture of Christmas carols, hymns, and local songs, with harmonies that reflect the rich vocal traditions of the Pacific. The choir performances often become the centerpiece of Christmas services, followed by communal feasts and celebrations.

Christmas in Oceania is as diverse and vibrant as the region itself, blending tropical landscapes with age-old traditions and island culture. Whether it's singing carols by candlelight in Australia, feasting on Pavlova in New Zealand, or watching millions of crabs migrate on Christmas Island, these festive customs highlight the joyful and community-focused nature of Christmas celebrations in the Pacific. Each tradition, rooted in local culture and shaped by the region's environment, reflects the warmth and spirit of Christmas in Oceania.

CHAPTER 7:

Unique and Uncommon Global Traditions

Around the world, Christmas is celebrated in ways that reflect local histories, beliefs, and environments. While some customs are widely known, others remain lesser-known yet equally fascinating. From Iceland's book-giving tradition to Vietnam's carols sung in rice paddies, these unique and uncommon global traditions offer a glimpse into how different cultures mark the holiday season.

1. Jolabokaflod – The Christmas Book Flood (Iceland)

In Iceland, Christmas is synonymous with books, thanks to the tradition of Jolabokaflod, or the Christmas Book Flood. This tradition dates back to World War II when paper was one of the few items not rationed. Icelanders began exchanging books as gifts on Christmas Eve, and it has since become a beloved tradition. On Christmas Eve, families gather to exchange books and spend the evening reading together. Jolabokaflod embodies the Icelandic love of literature and creates a cozy, peaceful start to Christmas.

2. Christmas Sauna (Finland, Estonia)

In Finland and Estonia, no Christmas is complete without a visit to the sauna. On Christmas Eve, many families heat their saunas in preparation for the holiday, as it is believed to cleanse both the body and the mind. The sauna is seen as a sacred place, and it's often said that the spirits of ancestors visit on this special day. After the sauna, families enjoy a festive meal and prepare for church services. The Christmas sauna is a time of relaxation, reflection, and purification before the holiday celebrations.

3. The Night of the Witches (Mexico)

In the small Mexican town of Catemaco, Christmas brings with it an unusual and mystical celebration known as La Noche de las Brujas (The Night of the Witches). On December 23rd, townspeople gather to celebrate the merging of local indigenous beliefs with Christian traditions. It's said that witches, healers, and shamans converge on the town during this time, performing rituals for good luck and protection in the coming year. While the tradition is deeply rooted in mysticism, it's also a lively and colorful event that reflects the blending of indigenous and Catholic practices in Mexico.

4. The Elves in the House (Norway)

In Norway, Nisse or Julenisse, small mythical creatures resembling elves, play an important role in Christmas folklore. It's believed that these elves protect homes and barns, but they also need to be kept happy with offerings of food. On Christmas Eve, Norwegian families leave out a bowl of porridge or rice pudding for the elves as a way to ensure their protection and goodwill in the coming year. The tradition reflects the blending of old Norse mythology with Christian Christmas celebrations.

5. Eating Fermented Shark (Iceland)

In Iceland, Christmas feasts sometimes feature an unusual and acquired taste: hákarl, or fermented shark. This dish, made from Greenland shark, is fermented for several months to remove toxins and then hung to dry. The result is a pungent and strong-smelling delicacy that is traditionally eaten during midwinter celebrations, including Christmas. While not everyone in Iceland includes hákarl in their holiday meals, it remains a symbol of the country's Viking heritage and resourceful culinary history.

6. Santa Lucia's Buns (Sweden)

In Sweden, the celebration of St. Lucia's Day on December 13th involves the baking of lussekatter, saffron-flavored buns shaped like an "S" and decorated with raisins. St. Lucia, the bringer of light during the dark Scandinavian winter, is honored with processions led by girls dressed in white robes, wearing crowns of candles. After the processions, families gather to share the warm, golden buns and drink glögg, a spiced wine. This tradition brings light and warmth to the long winter nights leading up to Christmas.

7. Christmas Spider Webs (Ukraine)

In Ukraine, one of the most unique Christmas tree decorations is the spider web. According to Ukrainian folklore, a poor widow and her children couldn't afford to decorate their Christmas tree, but on Christmas morning, they discovered it covered in beautiful, shimmering webs spun by spiders during the night. As the sunlight hit the webs, they turned to silver and gold. Today, Ukrainians decorate their trees with fake spider webs, believing that doing so brings good luck and fortune for the coming year.

8. Christmas Witches (Italy)

In Italy, the holiday season extends into Epiphany, celebrated on January 6th, when children eagerly await a visit from La Befana, the Christmas witch. According to legend, La Befana flies through the night on her broomstick, delivering gifts to children, much like Santa Claus. If children have been good, they'll receive sweets and presents in their stockings; if they've been naughty, they might find lumps of coal. The tradition of La Befana blends Italian folklore with Christian celebrations, making Epiphany a festive and magical end to the holiday season.

9. Carol Singing in Paddy Fields (Vietnam)

In Vietnam, Christmas caroling takes on a rural twist as carol singers often walk through the paddy fields of the countryside, serenading homes and villages with hymns and carols. Despite being a minority religion, Christmas is widely celebrated in Vietnam, particularly in urban centers, where decorations and festivities are common. In rural areas, carolers bring the Christmas spirit to the fields, symbolizing peace and goodwill as they sing to the farmers. The serene landscape of Vietnam provides a beautiful backdrop for this quiet and meaningful tradition.

10. St. Stephen's Day Horse Racing (Ireland)

In Ireland, St. Stephen's Day on December 26th is marked by a unique tradition: horse racing. The most famous event is the Leopardstown Christmas Festival, held just outside Dublin, where families gather to watch some of the best horse races of the season. St. Stephen's Day is also known for the Wren Boys tradition, where groups of people dress in colorful costumes and parade through towns, singing songs and playing music. These traditions are rooted in Irish folklore and the celebration of community during the holiday season.

11. Prawn Cocktails (Australia)

In Australia, Christmas is celebrated during the summer, and traditional meals are often swapped for seafood and salads. One dish that's particularly popular is the prawn cocktail, a classic appetizer made from fresh prawns served with a tangy cocktail sauce. Whether enjoyed at a barbecue on the beach or as part of a family meal at home, prawn cocktails have become a symbol of the Australian Christmas, reflecting the country's love of seafood and its laid-back holiday atmosphere.

CONCLUSION:

The Magic of Global Traditions

These unique and uncommon traditions from around the world show just how diverse and imaginative Christmas celebrations can be. Whether it's reading books by the fire in Iceland, singing carols in the paddy fields of Vietnam, or racing horses in Ireland, each tradition reflects the values, history, and creativity of the cultures that celebrate them. These customs remind us that while Christmas may look different around the globe, the spirit of joy, generosity, and community is universal.